The Phoenix Living Poets

A MAN IN MY POSITION

The Phoenix Living Poets

★

ALEXANDER BAIRD: *Poems*
ALAN BOLD: *To Find the New*
A Perpetual Motion Machine
GEORGE MACKAY BROWN: *The Year of the Whale*
JENNIFER COUROUCLI: *On this Athenian Hill*
GLORIA EVANS DAVIES: *Words – for Blodwen*
PATRIC DICKINSON: *This Cold Universe*
The World I see
D. J. ENRIGHT: *Addictions · The Old Adam*
Some Men are Brothers · Unlawful Assembly
JOHN FULLER: *Fairground Music*
The Tree that Walked
DAVID GILL: *Men Without Evenings*
J. C. HALL: *The Burning Hare*
MOLLY HOLDEN: *To Make Me Grieve*
JOHN HORDER: *A Sense of Being*
P. J. KAVANAGH: *On the Way to the Depot*
RICHARD KELL: *Control Tower*
LAURIE LEE: *The Sun my Monument*
LAURENCE LERNER: *The Directions of Memory*
CHRISTOPHER LEVENSON: *Cairns*
EDWARD LOWBURY: *Time for Sale · Daylight Astronomy*
NORMAN MACCAIG: *Measures · A Round of Applause*
A Common Grave · Surroundings · Rings on a Tree
JAMES MERRILL: *Nights and Days · Selected Poems*
RUTH MILLER: *Selected Poems*
LESLIE NORRIS: *Finding Gold*
ROBERT PACK: *Selected Poems*
ARNOLD RATTENBURY: *Second Causes*
ADRIENNE RICH: *Selected Poems*
JON SILKIN: *Nature with Man*
The Re-ordering of the Stones
JON STALLWORTHY: *Root and Branch*
GILLIAN STONEHAM: *When that April*
EDWARD STOREY: *North Bank Night*
TERENCE TILLER: *Notes for a Myth*
SYDNEY TREMAYNE: *The Swans of Berwick*
LOTTE ZURNDORFER: *Poems*

A MAN IN MY POSITION

by

NORMAN MACCAIG

CHATTO AND WINDUS

THE HOGARTH PRESS

1969

Published by
Chatto & Windus Ltd
with The Hogarth Press
42 William IV Street
London W.C.2.

★

Clarke, Irwin & Co. Ltd
Toronto

SBN 7012 0329 3

Printed in Great Britain by
William Lewis (Printers) Ltd Cardiff

CONTENTS

Numismatist

I think of you
in gold coins.
My thoughts of you, each one,
is a gold coin –
I am their miser but
they belong to you.

You think of me
as this and that and
something else.
But see me now –
blackjawed mediaeval smalltime crook
shaking gold coins in a bag
for the pinch of rich dust
left in the bottom.

Eyelashes of a Swan

The Chinese name for tea leaves.

My girl's more gaudy than a swan
though less gaudy than the Chinese name
for tea leaves.

More like that mandarin duck, that could be
camouflaged in some extraordinary place
no doubt; but here, circling
on the brew of a city pond,
she's a fizz, a splutter, an unconscious
fireworks display. Too exotic
to make her surroundings exotic,
she circles among the swans,
making them adjacent. They stare at her
with their formalised hauteur
out of eyes that – my unexotic mind
notices – are no more fringed with eyelashes
than with tea leaves.

Old Edinburgh

Down the Canongate
down the Cowgate
go vermilion dreams
snake's tongues of bannerets
trumpets with words from their mouths
saying Praise me, praise me.

Up the Cowgate
up the Canongate
lice on the march
tar on the amputated stump
Hell speaking with the tongue of Heaven
a woman tied to the tail of a cart.

And history leans by a dark entry
with words from his mouth
that say Pity me, pity me
but never forgive.

It's Hopeless

To see you from three places at once
is one of my impossible ambitions.
Rushing around you doesn't help
though I exhaust myself doing it.

Those mystical mathematicians
don't help either. I listen
to their fifth dimensions, I try
to pick up a piece of bent light –

and there you are, with no legs,
no breasts, no voice. How can I
take a formula to the movies
or lie in bed fondling an equation?

If only you could stand
in a row of three! – But then, what torments
of indecision before I'd give one of you
that golden that Freudian apple.

Spring Tide

So shrunk, so thin,
he sits by the fire
less a man
than a birdcage
in which wings still flutter
a little.

He seldom speaks. But sometimes
he remembers a thing
that happened in a sixty years ago
other world.

How he laughs with glee
when he tells how the butcher
anchored his dinghy, one Spring tide,
with a rope so short
it pulled the boat under.

It's the glee that hurts.
– Doesn't he realise
what he's saying?

Sure Proof

I can no more describe you
than I can put a thing for the first time
where it already is.

If I could make a ladder of light
or comb the hair of a dream girl with a real comb
or pour a table into a jug . . .

I'm not good at impossible things.
And that is why I'm sure
I will love you for my ever.

Young Girl

She's pretty enough, though not beautiful.
In the house she makes herself
useful, in an inconspicuous way.
This is the only way
in which she is conspicuous.

She reminds me
of a privet hedge I once saw
with scores of leaves folded over in tubes,
each with a chrysalis inside it.

I'd like to be there on that day
when suddenly she's flowered and clouded with butterflies
before they fly off
and leave her useful
and quiet
and pretty enough.

The Root of It

On the rug by the fire
a stack of vocabulary rose up, confidently
piling adjectives and nouns and
tiny muscular verbs, storey by storey,
till they reached
almost to the ceiling. The word at the bottom
was love.

I rushed from the room. I
did not believe it. Feverishly
I turned over the pages of the dictionary
to find the blank spaces
they had left behind them – and there they were,
terrible as eyesockets.

What am I to do? What
am I to do? For I know
that tall stack would collapse,
every word would fly back and fill
those terrible spaces,
if I could snatch that word
from the bottom of the pile – if
I could learn again
the meaning of love.

Cliff Top, East Coast

A trawler lounges North through a gorsebush
that blazes
between me and the horizon.

What horizon? I lay my head down
on the world
and there's a new one, the limit
of a jungle of grassblades.
On one of them, beautifully bent over
a foot from my face,
I watch a caterpillar
filing past.

Horizons are plenty.
I sit up, and there –
seagulls tinily soaring
against huge brown cliffs –
guided snowflakes.

I remember the so many people
dying of horizons, dying of a surfeit
of moderation;
and I think – Girl,
I'll write you a poem
that praises you so well
it'll glow in the dark.

A Man in My Position

Hear my words carefully.
Some are spoken
not by me, but
by a man in my position.

What right has he
to use my mouth? I hate him
when he touches you
the wrong way.

Yet he loves you also,
this appalling stranger
who makes windows of my eyes.
You see him looking out.

Until he dies
of my love for you
hear my words carefully –
for who is talking now?

Home Bird

The happiness that has taken up lodgings in me
has cousins and uncles.

Mine is a stay-at-home quiet-as-a-mouse
thing, that sitting by the fire,
sends her mind out on the tundras
of carpets, the icefalls of bookshelves,
the narrow savannahs of mantelpieces.

Sometimes a cousin visits her, smelling
of smoke and collapsed buildings,
jingling the bullets in his pocket. He upsets
the furniture with his shouting
and rushes off impatient in the morning.

Or an uncle reels in
bruised and grinning –
he passes out on the sofa and next morning
groans and won't get up.

She tidies around him
and sits by the fire, timorously
looking at him and feeling
not quite herself. But when he takes
his mad eyes away, she sings a little
and sends her mind out
over Congos of chintz and Eiger
curtains, avoiding only
that periscope space in the wall
and the grenades of doorknobs.

Limits

So far as we know
a dropped jar smashes
without noticing it.

Trample a flower;
it dies with no malediction.

Is the noise made by a star
as it burns like a heretic in space
a noise of agony? . . .

Three terrible things happened to me.
I'm here. I survived them.
I take this for granted, it's part
of my knowledge.

But what frightens me is
our knowledge goes,
so far as we know, only
so far as we know.

And I think, when molecules jump
from one figuration to another
they may not go hallelujahing into heaven
or howling into hell,
but
water becomes ice.

God in the Grass

The basking adder
looks at the world
with a softly beaming eye
as though he had created it.

Coiled round himself
in a sabbath stillness
he approves of everything, he knows
it is all good.

In heavenly contemplation
he lets the world
bask in his look.

(And how is he to know
the cries, the sad crying
that he is deaf to?)

Inarticulates

When I look at you,
I, who prove better than some
that there are ways of telling
what there are no ways of showing,
have no words to say to you.

You answer this silence with yours.

But your silence wins. For how can I fail
to love you more as I watch you
proving better than anyone
that there are ways of showing
what there are no ways of telling?

Concerto

Miss pianist bows her lovely back
under the hail of notes
that she's returning, slightly damaged,
to Beethoven.

The audience put on looks
of exquisite thoughtfulness. How lucky
to have a horseshoe
in the middle of your skull.

On the podium, the conductor
is a cobra half reared
from a basket. How stupid
not to know who's master.

Beethoven knows nothing of such things
ever since his deafness
became deaf.

Uncle Roderick

His drifter swung in the night
from a mile of nets
between the Shiants and Harris.

My boy's eyes watched
the lights of the fishing fleet – fireflies
on the green field of the sea.

In the foc's'le he gave me a bowl
of tea, black, strong and bitter,
and a biscuit you hammered
in bits like a plate.

The fiery curtain came up
from the blackness, comma'd with corpses.

Round Rhu nan Cuideagan
he steered for home, a boy's god
in seaboots. He found his anchorage
as a bird its nest.

In the kitchen he dropped
his oilskins where he stood.

He was strong as the red bull.
He moved like a dancer.
He was a cran of songs.

Gaelic Poet

He sits in his white house,
a gathering storm of song.

The room is uneasy; it never
takes its eyes off him.

It's waiting till he pours out from it
clear drops for iris and scabious,

harsh floods for the choked ditch,
floods for the lustful salmon

and lightnings that will skewer
black hearts to their midnight beds.

The room watches him. He watches
the bright world he will make brighter

and the dark world he will make brighter.
He is dark with unborn brightnesses.

Walking to Inveruplan

Glowing with answers in the aromatic dark,
I walk, so wise,
Under the final problem of lit skies.

I reach the bridge, where the road turns north to Stoer,
And there perch me
Under the final problem of a tree.

I'm in my Li Po mood. I've half a mind
To sit and drink
Until the moon, that's just arisen, should sink.

The whisky's good, it constellates. How wise
Can a man be,
I think, inside that final problem, me.

If you are short of answers, I've got them all
As clear as day . . .
I blink at the moon and put the bottle away

And then walk on (for there are miles to go
And friends to meet)
Above the final problem of my feet.

Old Myth, New Model

Because his girl
thought no more and no less of him
than of anybody else,
his love became a burden to him.
He couldn't get rid of it, he hated it.

Watch the gods when they seem
kind. For he came
to love the love he hated –
it was necessary for him, what
would he be without it?

And who doubts
Sisyphus, also, grew, in a horrible way,
to love his stone:
a double punishment.

One of the Many Days

I never saw more frogs
than once at the back of Ben Dorain.
Joseph-coated, they ambled and jumped
in the sweet marsh grass
like coloured ideas.

The river ran glass in the sun.
I waded in the jocular water
of Loch Lyon. A parcel of hinds
gave the V-sign with their ears, then
ran off and off till they were
cantering crumbs. I watched
a whole long day
release its miracles.

But clearest of all I remember
the Joseph-coated frogs
amiably ambling or
jumping into the air – like
coloured ideas
tinily considering
the huge concept of Ben Dorain.

Transformations

What a pity thoughts are only to be contained
inside a skull.

My thoughts of you
are a string ball inside a canister.

If I could hold one end and toss that ball
it would unwind till it reached you
however far away you were.

As it is, I've to make words of them
and write them down in a letter and send it off,
gay swallow, unerringly crossing oceans
to its nesting place – where it'll fly
into your mind and become
a ball of string in the prettiest
canister I ever did see.

No End, No Beginning

I

. . . And a moon fat as a butterball
Over the wet feathers of treetops;
Meadowsweet smelling of gray honey;
The sealoch bulged like a biceps
In a jersey sleeve of rocks . . .
When ever was there a beginning? –
Not of night and its furniture,
Its transcriptions, its cool décor;
Nor of thinking about it:
But when was there a beginning
Of this turbulent love
For a sea shaking with light
And lullabying ditchwater
And a young twig being grave
Against constellations – these –
And people, invisibly webbing
Countries and continents,
Weeping, laughing, being idle
And always, always
Moving from light to darkness and
To light: a furniture
Of what? – a transcription, a décor
Of Being, that hard abstract
Curled in the jelly of an eye
And webbed through constellations
And cities and deserts, and frayed
In the wet feathers of treetops.

2

On the track to Fewin I met
heaped hills – a still-life of enormous apples:
and an owl swivelling his face like a plate
in a fir tree: and a grassgreen beetle
like a walking brooch.

All themselves and all likenesses.

Or I peer down from a sea rock
through the sidling glass, the salty light,
and see in that downward world green Samoas
and swaying Ceylons.

Resemblance makes kinships. Your face,
girl in my mind, is the heir
of all the beautiful women there have been.
I look and dazzle with the loveliness
of women I've never known.

And your hand is as cool as moonlight
and as gentle.

Such a web of likenesses. No matter
how many times removed, I am cousin
to volcanoes and leafbuds, and the heron
devouring a frog eats a bloodbrother of
suns and gravestones.

3

When you, in your unimaginable self,
suddenly were there, shut boxes opened

and worlds flew out coloured like picture books
and full of heavy lethargies and gay dances:

when I met a tree, my old familiar, I knew
this was the first time I was meeting it;

and the birds in it singing – for the first time
I could crack the code of their jargon.

And the boredom and loneliness
in the lit rooms of monotonous streets became

terrible and pitiful – you made me a member
of the secret society of humanity.

The future that had been failing muscles,
sagging flesh, cindering eyes –

all mine, all only mine – swarmed in the air
and spread its new meaning back

into every yesterday. Flux, revolution
emerged into sense, into their own

explanations. I could understand them,
not wholly, but I could understand them

as I could know, not wholly, the meaning
of your still hand, quiet look, a way of walking

that takes you from the first garden to the future
where the apple hangs, still, on its dangerous tree.

4

The dinghy across the bay
Puts out two hands and swims
An elegant backstroke over
A depth full of images.

A gull swings round a rock,
Glides by. No feathers stir –
Dead still as a living fossil
In a geology of air.

I pick a round grassblade
And chew it. The sap breeds
A campfire, dark figures, a blackness
Full of dangerous woods.

And in that tree, that house,
That girl on the gray rocks,
That wave – in everything
A vigorous future kicks.

He'll be born, full of graves,
Greedy and angry. His screams
Will fill us with an ancient pity.
He'll lie helpless in our arms.

Old Rose Bush

In this salt air, the wild rose bush
is a tatter from the root up, is
a diagram from which
most lines have been erased

With straight lines and obtuse
angles it explores
the three visible dimensions
and produces from the fourth
one rose.

It stands like a beggar
at the corner of the road –
skinny old seaman with
a parakeet on his shoulder.

Shifts

I walked you away from three corners.
Why do you want to feel trapped?
When I ask you why you pretend love is cruel,
you say, In case it is.

I walk you into a cornerless place
and say, Look, if there's nowhere to run to,
there's nothing to run from. But you stare wildly around
and run and run till you come
to that fourth corner, and from it
you beckon me, smiling
at last with love. Do you pretend
I'm your trapper, your hunter,
in case I am?

Be careful. These shifts
so tire me out I wonder
if I'm only pretending to love you
in case I do.

Spilled Salt

A salt hill
the size it is
because I'm the size I am.

Suilven (that mountain)
since it notices nothing
takes its size from me . . .

That grief I suffered
when she died
was made to my measure.

I loved her, I mourned her
with all the love I had,
with all the grief I had.

She whose look
gave me the size
I thought I was

became spilled salt;
for she
had stopped noticing.

I look at her image.
I hate it.
I sweep it away.

Next Day

That hill was not there this morning.
We walked on what it used to be
and changed it to this.

As: I sit in what was my room
practically dangling my feet
over a cloud-edge,
almost playing a harp –
but not, thank God,
quite.

Or: take a blank sheet of paper.
I'd stare at one
trying to populate it
with vivacious words. What a business
to assemble a few couples and groups!
But this one – it swarmed
with festivals and Bank Holidays.
And what a job I've had
to drive away the crowds at the side
and let through
this procession going down the middle.

Types

He pokes his ant-eater face
into the crannies between feelings
and writes about them as if they were
a soft geology.

His colleague dips a toe
into the meniscus of four faiths
and betrays them all. If only
he'd wet even his kneebones.

Their lady colleague turns slums and jungles
into delicate plastic orchards
whose lack of scent she bottles
in beautiful bottles.

A list that could go on: people
more freakish than pangolins
or sauntering seahorses
they write a new Aesop's Fable

in a world where villages are
burning Bethlehems
and love grows stronger only
from its long weeping.

Confession

He lifts a waggish finger
and glassfuls of poems
shake in the light.

That other draws down his brows
and disastrous wings
fan their terrible shadows
over whole landscapes.

I envy him. For my
brows and my fingers are worked
by the same mechanism.
When I draw down the one
the other wags.

Too happy to be sad. What
a pleasant, what a terrible
exclusion.

By a Water

The sky was wet zinc.
Waves snuffled along the low cliffs –
what were they longing to get at?

You spoke words
that turned into wounds. I was guilty
only of being me.

The sky came down on my eyes.
I stared at the world
through a web of zinc.

And inside me something went snuffling,
searching for a victim
to lay at your feet.

Mrs. Grant

She was a wild one, clutching in a fist
Made of green fingers once whole crews of lost
Norwegian sailors drunk till half past four
And up at six each with a woodpecker
Inside his skull. She bred her blacktongued chows
And starved them, and the Jerseys, while the glass
Of gin was filled and filled. Pigeons and doves
Tumbled about the turrets; goats scavenged leaves
And rags and woodchips; on the lawn's half-ring
A jackboot peacock strutted, suffering
Its self-inflicted cries.

One day she walked
Medusa-haired into the sea but hooked
Her dirty nails on life and back she splashed –
A picture Botticelli didn't paint.
Then drugs, of course, and fat policemen not
Knowing what to do, screams in the village street,
Coals on the carpet, dishes moulded blue
And lengthening notes from the RSPCA.
A Greek doom gathered round, the Furies whetted
Their ugly beaks and one by one alighted
On the rooftree . . . What of her was seen last
Through the cracked windscreen of her blue Ford Eight
Was a bruised cheek, a wild and staring eye . . .
Her house (it's true) was called Society.

Basking Shark

To stub an oar on a rock where none should be,
To have it rise with a slounge out of the sea
Is a thing that happened once (too often) to me.

But not too often – though enough. I count as gain
That once I met, on a sea tin-tacked with rain,
That roomsized monster with a matchbox brain.

He displaced more than water. He shoggled me
Centuries back – this decadent townee
Shook on a wrong branch of his family tree.

Swish up the dirt and, when it settles, a spring
Is all the clearer. I saw me, in one fling,
Emerging from the slime of everything.

So who's the monster? The thought made me grow pale
For twenty seconds while, sail after sail,
The tall fin slid away and then the tail.

No Wizard, No Witch

  Watch the sky clear:
I wave my hand – and clouds crowd grumbling up.
  You want a rose? Why, yes –
I wave my hand and there's a wilderness.
I offer wine in my most splendid cup;
What reaches you? A mug of flattish beer.

  You give me a stone –
It preens and sings in Yeats's Byzantium.
  And when you say Goodnight
It turns to lyrics Shakespeare failed to write.
You give me a garden (it's one chrysanthemum):
And your hand's a consort, with every flute a bone.

  Not fair, not fair.
My brain cracks trying to please you, muttering
  New and ancestral spells . . .
It's your transfiguring innocence that tells
A stone to be a bird – or, a stranger thing,
The actual air to be the actual air.

So Many Summers

Beside one loch, a hind's neat skeleton,
Beside another, a boat pulled high and dry:
Two neat geometries drawn in the weather:
Two things already dead and still to die.

I passed them every summer, rod in hand,
Skirting the bright blue or the spitting gray,
And, every summer, saw how the bleached timbers
Gaped wider and the neat ribs fell away.

Time adds one malice to another one –
Now you'd look very close before you knew
If it's the boat that ran, the hind went sailing.
So many summers, and I have lived them too.

Nothing's Enough

That flesh you're proud of, those eyes,
Live aquamarines – they're masks,
Inventions, they're not there.
What's fungus and what's bright hair?
Put a ring on your finger: it clicks.

You touch me. You think so?
I'm smoke, I'm thickened space,
I'm something you invented.
– Yet I'm touched, I have to say it,
By that rigmarole of bones.

I love your transparency
On the dark wall of my mind –
I dote on you, lovely landscape
Of brittleness, blueprint of sleep,
Diagram of the world's end.

I undress you of your proud flesh
And see your thoughts thinking,
But you – a woman? We speak
Like pages rustling, we walk
As though towers of words were walking.

Nearness isn't enough,
My foreign land. You come
In cantos and shapes of colour
That dizzy my mind with pleasure,
But I sleep in your body's dream.

Lift up that claw and clothe it:
It says you're somewhere – but long
Spaces away; and gently
I touch, not you, but only
Sweet flesh and a clinking ring.

Reclining Figure by Henry Moore: Botanic Gardens, Edinburgh

It was the place that it was in
And was in what the place was. So,
Its dinosaurish head poked out
Into the twentieth century.

It seemed as though it had been left,
Denying momentariness,
A glacial deposit, by
A geology of ancestors.

Yet it was, too, one mass of these
Douce citizens sprawled on the grass –
See them, ferocious ratepayers
Flirting with lovely dinosaurs.

Green Stain

A filth of leaves, she said, a froth, she said
Of sudsy flowers, and there's your mawkish Spring.
Oh, barebone tree, what has it done to you?
Black field, you're gone but for remembering.

I keep my winter where my heart should be.
– I'd rather bear it in its blackest moods
Than see those frilly leaves and blossoms make
A haberdashery of wholesome woods.

A mish-mash green, a sickly groping, such
A fumbling into light! How could they surpass
The icy shapes of darling winter hidden
In luckless trees and ill-starred meadow grass?

Structures

Stand in this shade and think of me as me –
The moon's a pedant of the present tense
And I'm recessions, my own short history.

I changed before you changed me, as you must
Be differences in this moment's mode:
Stars once were gases or exploding dust.

I'm no forever. My tomorrow's man,
Necrophilous of me, will all the same
Have bridged a crack that only I could span.

I'll grin with new jaws in your smiling face,
That dulcet resurrection, but not forget
The one I now see in this moment's place.

Don't tie me down in it. Recession has
Its gifts to give, though some of them to guess –
Being differences hard for logic, as

The great world leader was a schoolboy dunce,
A sandgrain was a hilltop and – look up –
That moon's blood orange was a cat's claw once.

Drop Scene

Fit for a pantomime, my familiar landscape,
Now tiny twigs are flocculent with snow
And walls are coped with it and fields stare white –
A good place for Bad Uncles to recite
Atrocious rhymes to the Princess and her beau.

Through this goosefeathery water real water
Runs inky black. It made a chuckling sound
But now it sobs under its breath, slipping
Beneath gold streaks of the moon. And no birds sing
Under a sky whose clouds have gone to ground.

That's where mine are. I watch their level whiteness
Comforting seeds that will make a new Spring day.
Yet though it's in its pretty winter time
My mind's made sad, too sad for pantomime,
By that one line of footprints going away.

Things in their Elements

Ten thousand starlings in the air
Right-turn as one, as one go soaring.
A pear-shaped shoal of baby herring
In shallow water does the same.

Who gave them orders is your boss.
For when I watch your thousand graces
They move as one – not even two inches
Act as a tiny awkward squad.

The links of things! I cross the room
And influence tides; a hopping sparrow
Gives a small shog to the centre
Of gravity in Betelgeuse.

I move, he moves, they move – and, given
An eye that's sharp enough and subtle,
You'd notice how at every gesture
The earth stutters going through heaven.

But you're a friend of gravity,
With such accommodation (its nature's
Love) the sensitive, huge planet
Dozes on dreamlessly through space.

Not me, though, I'm all earthquakes – they
Stand fallen trees up and rebuild ruins.
My seismograph's gone crazy: proving
Your element is more than air.

Descent from the Green Corrie

The climb's all right, it's the descent that kills you.
Knees become fists that don't know how to clench
And thighs are strings in parallel.
Gravity's still your enemy: it drills you
With your own backbone – its love is all to wrench
You down on screes or boggy asphodel.

And the elation that for a moment fills you
Beside the misty cairn's that lesser thing,
A memory of it. It's not
The punishing climb, it's the descent that kills you
However sweetly the valley thrushes sing
And shadows darken with the peace they've brought.

Venus Fly-trap

Ridding my mind of cant
With one deft twist of my most deep convictions,
I find you are less animal than plant.

You suck the rank soil in
And flourish, on your native commonplaces,
The lively signal of a sense of sin.

I buzzed and landed, but,
Encroaching with my loving bumbling fumble,
Found the whole world go black. The trap was shut.

Now in your juices, I
Am helpless to give warning to my rivals
And, worse, have to digest them when they die.

And worst, since now I'm one
Of your true converts, what is all my labour? –
To flaunt your signals in the shocking sun.

A Man in Assynt

Glaciers, grinding West, gouged out
these valleys, rasping the brown sandstone,
and left, on the hard rock below – the
ruffled foreland –
this frieze of mountains, filed
on the blue air – Stac Polly,
Cul Beag, Cul Mor, Suilven,
Canisp – a frieze and
a litany.

Who owns this landscape?
Has owning anything to do with love?
For it and I have a love-affair, so nearly human
we even have quarrels. –
When I Intrude too confidently
it rebuffs me with a wind like a hand
or puts in my way
a quaking bog or a loch
where no loch should be. Or I turn stonily
away, refusing to notice
the rouged rocks, the mascara
under a dripping ledge, even
the tossed, the stony limbs waiting.

I can't pretend
it gets sick for me in my absence,
though I get
sick for it. Yet I love it
with special gratitude, since
it sends me no letters, is never
jealous and, expecting nothing
from me, gets nothing but
cigarette packets and footprints.

Who owns this landscape? –
The millionaire who bought it or
the poacher staggering downhill in the early morning
with a deer on his back?

Who possesses this landscape? –
The man who bought it or
I who am possessed by it?

False questions, for
this landscape is
masterless
and intractable in any terms
that are human.
It is docile only to the weather
and its indefatigable lieutenants –
wind, water and frost.
The wind whets the high ridges
and stunts silver birches and alders.
Rain falling down meets
springs gushing up –
they gather and carry down to the Minch
tons of sour soil, making bald
the bony scalp of Cul Mor. And frost
thrusts his hand in cracks and, clenching his fist,
bursts open the sandstone plates,
the armour of Suilven:
he bleeds stones down chutes and screes,
smelling of gunpowder.

Or has it come to this,
that this dying landscape belongs
to the dead, the crofters and fighters
and fishermen whose larochs
sink into the bracken
by Loch Assynt and Loch Crocach? –
to men trampled under the hoofs of sheep

and driven by deer to
the ends of the earth – to men whose loyalty
was so great it accepted their own betrayal
by their own chiefs and whose descendants now
are kept in their place
by English businessmen and the indifference
of a remote and ignorant government.

Where have they gone, the people
who lived between here and
Quinag, that tall
huddle of anvils that puffs out
two ravens into the blue and
looks down on the lochs of Stoer
where trout idle among reeds and
waterlilies – take one of them home
and smell, in a flower,
the sepulchral smell of water.

Beyond Fewin lies the Veyatie Burn – fine
crossing place for deer, they trot over
with frills of water flouncing
at their knees. That water rests in Fewin
beneath the sandstone hulk
of Suilven, not knowing what's to come –
the clattering horserush down
the Kirkaig gorge, the sixty-foot
Falls . . . There are twenty-one pools
on the Kirkaig . . . Since
before empires were possible
till now, when so many have died
in their own dust,
the Kirkaig Falls have been walking backwards –
twenty-one paces up their own stream.
Salmon lie
in each of the huge footprints.

You can try to catch them –
at a price.
The man whose generations of ancestors
fished this, their own river,
can catch them still –
at a price . . .

The salmon come from the sea. I watch
its waves thumping down their glossy arches in
a soup of sand, folding over from one
end of the bay to the other.
Sandpipers, ringed plover, turnstones
play tig with these waves that
pay no heed but laboriously get on with
playing their million-finger exercises on
the keyboard of the sand.

The salmon come from the sea. Men
go out on it. The *Valhalla,* the *Golden Emblem*
come in, smoking with gulls,
from the fishing grounds of the Minch
to lie, docile, by the Culag pier.
Beneath it the joppling water
shuffles its blues and greens till they almost
waver the burly baulks away.
From the tall bows ropes reach ashore
in languid arcs, till, through rings, round
bollards, they clot and
twist themselves in savage knots.
The boats lie still with a cargo
of fish and voyages.

Hard labour can relax.
The salty smell outside, which is made up
of brine and seaweed
and fish, reaches the pub door but
is refused admittance. Here,

men in huge jerseys drink small drinks.
The thick talk
of fishing and sheep is livened
by a witty crackle of gossip
and the bitter last tale
of local politics. At ten o'clock, the barman
will stop whistling a strathspey to shout
"Time, please!" and they
will noisily trail out, injecting a guff of alcohol
into the salty smell made up
of brine and seaweed
and fish, which stretches from the pub door
all the way to America.

Whom does the sea belong to?
Fat governments? Guillemots? Or men
who steal from it what they can
to support their dying acres?

Fish from the sea, for Glasgow, London,
Edinburgh. But the land, too, sells
itself; and from these places
come people tired of a new civilisation
to taste what's left
of an old one. They outnumber
the locals – a thing
too easy to do . . . In Lochinver,
Achmelvich, Clashnessie, Clachtoll
they exchange the tyranny of the clock
for the natural rhythm of day and
night and day and night and for
the natural decorum that binds together
the fishing grounds, crofting lands
and the rough sheepruns that hoist themselves
towards the hills. They meet the people
and are not rejected. In the sweating night
London and Edinburgh fall away

under the bouncing rhythms of *Strip the Willow*
and the *Gay Gordons,* and when the lights go out
and all the goodnights are spoken, they can hear
a drunk melodeon go without staggering
along the dark road.

But the night's not over. A twinkle of light
in Strathan, Brackloch, Inveruplan, shows
where the tales are going round, tall
as the mast of the *Valhalla,* and songs are sung
by keeper, shepherd and fisherman,
each tilting his Rembrandt face in the light
and banging the chorus round, till, with a shout
he takes up his dram and drinks it down.
The Gauger of Dalmore lives again
in verses. An old song
makes history alive again,
as a rickle of stones peoples the dark theatre
of the mind with a shouting crowd and,
in the middle, MacLeod of Assynt and
his greater prisoner – Montrose.

An old song. A rickle of stones. A
name on a map.
I read on a map a name whose Gaelic means
the Battlefield of the Big Men.
I think of yelling hosts, banners,
counterattacks, deployments. When I get there,
it's ten acres, ten small acres
of boggy ground.
I feel
I am looking through the same wrong end
of the same telescope
through which I look back through time
and see
Christ, Socrates, Dante – all the Big Men
picked out, on their few acres,

clear and tiny in
the misty landscape of history.

Up from that mist crowds
the present. This day has lain long,
has dozed late, till
the church bell jerks and, wagging madly
in its salty tower, sends its voice
clanking through the sabbath drowse.
And dark minds in black clothes gather like
bees to the hive, to share
the bitter honey of the Word, to submit
to the hard judgment of a God
my childhood God would have a difficulty
in recognising.
Ten yards from the sea's surge
they sing to Him beautiful praises
that surge like the sea,
in a bare stone box built
for the worship of the Creator
of all colours and between-colours, and of
all shapes, and of the holiness
of identity and of the purifying light-stream
of reason. The sound of that praise
escapes from the stone box
and takes its place in the ordinary communion
of all sounds, that are
Being expressing itself – as it does in its continuous,
its never-ending creation of leaves,
birds, waves, stone boxes – and beliefs,
the true and the false.

These shapes, these incarnations, have their own determin
identities, their own dark holiness, their
high absurdities. See how they make
a breadth and assemblage of animals, a
perpendicularity of creatures, from where,

three thousand feet up, two ravens go by
in their seedy, nonchalant way, down to
the burn-mouth where baby mussels
drink fresh water through their beards –
or down, down still, to where the masked conger eel
goes like a gangster through
the weedy slums at the sea's foot.

Greenshank, adder, wildcat, guillemot, seatrout,
fox and falcon – the list winds through
all the crooks and crannies of this landscape, all
the subtleties and shifts of its waters and
the prevarications of its air –
while roofs fall in, walls crumble, gables
die last of all, and man becomes,
in this most beautiful corner of the land,
one of the rare animals.

Up there, the scraping light
whittles the cloud edges till, like thin bone,
they're bright with their own opaque selves. Down here,
a skinny rosebush is an eccentric jug
of air. And I,
somewhere between them,
am a visiting eye,
an unrequited passion,
watching the tide glittering backward and making
its huge withdrawal from beaches
and kilted rocks. And the mind
behind the eye, within the passion,
remembers with certainty that the tide will return
and thinks, with hope, that that other ebb,
that sad withdrawal of people, may, too,
reverse itself and flood
the bays and the sheltered glens
with new generations, replenishing the land
with its richest of riches and coming, at last,
into their own again.

Prisoner

You think you can take me from your pocket
and show me to your friends like a pebble you've found.
You're wrong.
You lock me in a cell without windows
but where am I when you open the door again?
Do you think you can point to me
stuffed beside the coathangers or lift a lid
and say, "See, Norman in aspic"?
That thing in your buttonhole –
do you really, truly think it's me?

On the other hand, when you go alone to bed,
whose voice whispers from the pillow beside you?
You open a newspaper and it's a street
with me walking along it.
When you put your hand in your handbag
another hand grasps it –
it's mine.
When you mean to say "God".
it's my name comes from your mouth. When you mean to
"Hell", it's my name comes from your mouth.

It's not my helplessness that makes me your prisoner,
it's yours.

Space Fiction

I said the word "spatial", and in it
a micro-universe created itself, whirling
and fizzing and letting off
inaudible explosions.

I said "akimbo" and in it a crowd of
Chinamen doubled over with laughing in
every direction.

I said "seven" and there was a perspective
of gibbets, each with a little 7
hung from a rope's end.

I said "semantic space" – and a macro-universe
was filled, was a plenum of identical
images of you.

I risked it, I said "you", and the word
burst. I watched its expanding universe,
its continuous creation, dangling akimbo
amongst inaudible explosions.

The Unlikely

I dropped a bottle on a stone –
and the stone broke.
A friend (drunk) fell from the top box in the theatre
and landed in the second top one. Impossible.

We like the unlikely. It's good
that the boundaries of the normal should be widened.
It means – how many things there are still to be noticed!

A mistake in a laboratory –
and there's penicillin.
Throw a stone into a cave and what do you get?
The Dead Sea Scrolls.

We like the unlikely. The terrible thing is
we like it, too, when it's terrible.
When the quiet clerk poisons his family,
when the doctor says Cancer, when the tanks
clank on the innocent frontier,
inside the fear, the rage and the horror
a tiny approval smirks, ashamed of itself.

That tiny approval has murdered more people
than Genghis Khan. It widened the boundaries of the norm
with the explosion over Hiroshima.

That means – how many things there are still to be
suffered!

Wild Oats

Every day I see from my window
pigeons, up on a roof ledge – the males
are wobbling gyroscopes of lust.

Last week a stranger joined them, a snowwhite
pouting fantail,
Mae West in the Women's Guild.
What becks, what croo-croos, what
demented pirouetting, what a lack
of moustaches to stroke.

The females – no need to be one of them
to know
exactly what they were thinking – pretended
she wasn't there
and went dowdily on with whatever
pigeons do when they're knitting.

Dancing Minister

In a one-two-three
she waltzes by, big as a brigantine.

Her tug, with a red-hot smokestack,
is short of tonnage, is short of horsepower.

She has no visible means
of propulsion. She drifts
curvaceously on
invisible swirlings and eddies.

A passing tug hails them: "Minister,
what would St. Luke think of you now?"

The parson sweats. Theology
was nothing to this.

Power Dive

He spent a fortune on architects and builders.
He signed tickertapes of cheques for furniture,
carpets, paintings, filmstar beds. He surrounded the house
with plantations and parterres, hahas and gazebos.
And in the right place, the properest place
at last he saw completed a swimmingpool
that glittered like ancient Rome.

It was just before he hit the water
in his first dive that he glimpsed
the triangular fin cutting the surface.

Academic

You sit at your fat desk, starching
your brains; you're the tone-deaf man
in the orchestra, you're the frog
who wouldn't a-wooing go.

What a job is this, to measure
lightning with a footrule, the heart's
turbulence with a pair of callipers.
And what a magician, who can
dismantle Juliet, Ahab, Agememnon
into a do-it-yourself kit
of semantic gestures.

Tidiness is decent. Trains
have to reach their destinations.
But yours, that should be
clattering and singing
through villages and landscapes, never
get out of the shunting yards.

I'm a simple man – I believe
you were born, I believe it
against all the evidence.
I would like to give you
a present of weather, a
transfusion of pain.

In My Mind

I go back ways to hurl rooftops
into that furze-blazing sunset.

I stare at water
frilling a stone, flexing a muscle.

Down sidestreets I sniff
cats in passages, old soup and

in one hot room
the fierce smell of hyacinths.

From the tops of spires
I lasso two counties in an eye-blink

and break my ears with a jukebox
in a frowsy cellar.

I am an honorary citizen
of these landscapes and a City Father

of this city. I walk
through its walls and burn

as traffic lights. It is all
lines on my hand.

But I turn away
from that terrible cul de sac.

I turn away from
the smiling house there

and the room in it
with green blinds drawn

and a bed with a bed lamp shedding
its kind light down

on a dead hand
and a book fallen from it.

World within World

When a thin cloud goes over
it drops a shadow on the bed of the rock pool
like a reflection of smoke.

It doesn't disturb
the glinting fish-needles, the bazaar jungles
of weed, the hermit crab's
preposterous claws.

But if I break the water surface
with a finger tip, what dartings
and scuttlings and tiny fountains
of sand. Gods are alright
if they stay in heaven.

I glance up, idiotically imagining
bright ripples on the blue and the tip
of a huge forefinger. – It's more difficult
than that. How escape
a god who disguises himself
as me being god observing
himself disguised as
a hermit crab, three whelks and
a pouting anemone?